Answer THE CALL

Discovering and answering the call of God that is on your life

Debrecia Echols

Answer THE CALL

Discovering and answering the call of God that is on your life

Debrecia Echols

T&J PUBLISHERS

A SMALL INDEPENDENT PUBLISHER WITH A BIG VOICE

Printed in the United States of America by
T&J Publishers (Atlanta, GA.)
www.TandJPublishers.com

© Copyright 2019 by Debrecia Echols

All rights reserved. This book or parts thereof may not be reproduced in any form, stored in a retrieval system, or transmitted in any form by any means-electronic, mechanical, photocopy, recording, or otherwise-without prior written permission of the author, except as provided by United States of America copyright law.

Cover Design by Timothy Flemming, Jr. (T&J Publishers)
Book Format/Layout by Timothy Flemming, Jr.

ISBN: 978-1-7335470-1-7

To contact author, go to:
debrecia@outlook.com
Facebook: Debrecia Echols
Instagram: @debrecia
Twitter: @debrecia_echols

I dedicate this to my Lord and Savior Jesus Christ and all my family that has gone before me. May these encounters open up your heart!

"For whom he did foreknow, he also did predestinate to be conformed to the image of his Son, that he might be the firstborn among many brethren. Moreover whom he did predestinate, them he also called: and whom he called, them he also justified: and whom he justified, them he also glorified."
—Romans 8:29-30

TABLE OF CONTENTS

Introduction	11
Entry 1: The Call	13
Entry 2: Draw Me Nearer	21
Entry 3: God's Hand Revealed	29
Entry 4: The Trust Game	37
Entry 5: Your Miracle Is Here	43
Entry 6: Lucifer	51
Entry 7: My Visit To Hell	57
Entry 8: A Place Called Heaven	63
Entry 9: A Child Found	69
Entry 10: God Disappointed	75
Entry 11: In My Face	81
Entry 12: An Angel At My Door	87
Entry 13: Angelic Intervention	93
Entry 14: Angels Singing With Us	99
Entry 15: Heaven Invading The Room	105
Entry 16: A Heart For Africa	111
Entry 17: God Shows Me Africa	117
Entry 18: My Calling Revealed	123

Introduction

NOTHING HAPPENS BY CHANCE WITH ME. I KNOW that some of these encounters would scare people, but I had to be obedient and write them down. For these things are true and they are an accurate account of my encounters with God, His angels, and even entities from the demonic realm.

I encourage you to read a different journal entry each day. Don't just read the journal entries, but ponder them in your heart and spend time reflecting on the messages given. Take time to write down your thoughts in the journal sections and engage in the Your Time To Reflect exercises. This will maximize your experience of reading this book and help you to discover God's calling for your life.

Let's get started!

ANSWER THE CALL

Journal Entry #1

The Call

"For many are called, but few are chosen."—Matthew 22:14

Have you ever felt like you were different from others, but you couldn't quite put your finger on what makes you different? Have you ever felt like an oddball, and like you can't fit in with the crowd? That's me. That's how I felt for most of my life. I couldn't understand why I felt this way until I began having supernatural encounters at a young age. It all started when one day I heard the voice of God—He spoke to me and revealed to me that I was knitted together in my mother's womb for such a time as this.

My life was always unique. For three months the Doctors could not explain why my mother was not having her cycle. She knew she was pregnant, but no heartbeat could be detected in her womb. Everyone was puzzled, including my dad. I figure God needed a little extra time forming me in my mother's womb because of the purpose and assignment He has placed on my life. However, as David revealed, all of us were wonderfully and fearfully made by God. We were all fashioned by God in our mothers' wombs. You're unique. I'm unique. We're all unique.

Mom's pregnancy with me was different from her pregnancy with her other children. For about three months my mother didn't have a cycle, and she went to the doctor to find out why. The Doctor repeatedly told my parents that they couldn't detect a heartbeat in her womb; therefore she was not pregnant. "But how can that be?" they wondered. No menstrual cycle for three months! That's not normal; and then, mysteriously, after the third month, there I appeared. The doctor was speechless, left trying to figure out how my mom knew she was pregnant although there were no visible signs of pregnancy. It's as if I was hidden in my mom's womb. Sometimes, God will hide us when He's preparing to do something incredible in and through us. He'll hide us like He did Moses when Pharaoh's men were after him like He did Jesus when Herod's men were after Him like He did David when King Saul and his men were after him. Don't get upset when it seems as if God has hidden you from the spotlight, from the public, for the moment. He may be protecting you while preparing you for something great. Just because you answer the call of God upon your life, that doesn't mean He instantly and immediately presents you before the public. Sometimes, He may keep you hidden, concealed, like a secret weapon waiting for the perfect moment to be unleashed.

One minute, no one saw me in my mother's womb.

THE CALL

Months had gone by, and I couldn't be found. I didn't appear on the radar. There were no signs that I was even in my mother's womb. Suddenly, three months later I appeared seemingly out of nowhere on the sonogram. Right then, my mother realized that there was something special about me. Years later, when I reached the age of seventeen, my parents tried to explain to me everything that happened regarding my birth. As my dad explained everything to me, I was blown away. I was almost as shocked as he was at how everything happened. I realized then that my birth was something strange.

Back in those days, I suppose that it was a little too much to believe in the supernatural for many people, but with God, all things are possible the Bible tells us. God had a plan for my life even way back then. He was doing something in the spiritual that didn't make sense in the natural. His hand was on the whole situation.

Finally, I was born Debrecia Roteil Brazil on December 1, 1978, in the small town of Thomaston, Georgia. My parents were young when they had me. Mom was 17 years old, and dad was 21. My mom's mother, Maxine, named me since my parents were indecisive about what to call me.

I was a strange child with cat-like eyes that would change colors from time to time. Mom said that I'd always been different since I was born. I was the child that ran from cameras. I never liked taking pictures, and I hated dressing up, but these aren't the things that made me different. The thing that made me unique was my supernatural experiences with God.

From the age of eight, I'd have supernatural encounters with the Lord. No, these aren't hallucinations or dreams;

they're real encounters I've had with the Lord. Jesus is alive, and I've seen Him for myself. I've also seen Heaven and Hell as the Lord has shown me these things. They are as real as you and me! I've seen people in Heaven like the daughter I lost back in 2008, and I've seen other family members in Hell. These things I've written down. These things, the Lord has impressed upon my heart to share with others for the sake of strengthening their faith and providing them with hope and insight into the unseen reality of the spirit world. That's what this book is about.

God is real! Jesus is real! Heaven and Hell are real! The afterlife is real! Real consequences and rewards are awaiting every soul in the afterlife. Moreover, God is calling your name while there is still time for you to answer. Answer the call. You can hear it, sense it, feel it. Please don't put it off and ignore it. Heed His voice today and say yes to Him. Give Him your life, your heart, your soul, your all and all. He's waiting.

Your Time To Reflect

1. In what ways are you unique?

THE CALL

2. How have you sensed the call of God upon your life?

Additional Notes

Additional Notes

Additional Notes

Journal Entry #2
Draw Me Nearer

"Draw nigh to God, and he will draw nigh to you."
—James 4:8

My My family and I attended an African Methodist Episcopal (AME) Church in Thomaston, Georgia. That church has a rich history. Slaves attended that church. My younger sister and I would go to Vacation Bible School (VBS) during the summer months. My great-grandmother made sure we were in Sunday School every Sunday. Special services like Easter Sunday were especially important. We'd dress up in our best on those occasions. We stayed in church. As a child, I was groomed to seek after God with all of my heart. So although I had not yet had a supernatural visitation from the Lord, I spent my childhood learning of Him and seeking Him through His Word, learning how to experience His presence during worship and how to talk to Him from my heart during prayer. Even still, my heart longed for a supernatural encounter with God. I would hear others talk about their supernatural encounters with Christ-like my aunt, Shelia.

One day, aunt Shelia invited the whole family to a Sunday night church service at her church. During the service, while the pastor was inviting those in need of prayer to the altar, I got up out of my seat and headed to that altar. The pastor asked me if I wanted to accept Jesus as my Lord and Savior and I said yes. That night, my whole family approached the altar during the altar call for prayer and salvation—there was my mother, my aunts, my grandmother, and my little cousins. We all stood there lined up in a row. While at that altar, I could sense that something was getting ready to happen. The Pastor prayed for me, and I asked Jesus into my heart. Immediately after the prayer, the Holy Spirit came upon me. I then found myself speaking in an unknown tongue, and it felt like a fire was burning on the inside of me. The whole experience was incredible.

As a teenager, I would see clouds appearing inside of the church's sanctuary while worship was taking place. I would later discover that those clouds I'd see were the manifest glory of God. I believed at the time that everyone was seeing what I was seeing, but they weren't. I didn't know anything about the seer anointing and being gifted to see in the spirit realm. I would only hear about certain people like the Native American descendants who would often see and interact with spirits, but I didn't discover until much later that my family had a strong history of these kinds of experiences.

I began having all kind of supernatural experiences.

During certain times in church, I would feel wind blowing, and suddenly people would start falling out under the power of God. God was giving me signs of His existence. I began having encounters with Him right after this. God began to speak to me. At eight years old, my life changed, and I would never be the same.

Your Time To Reflect

1. What signs have God shown you that proves His existence is real?

2. As I discovered as a child, the more we seek God, the more He draws close to us and reveals Himself to us. In what ways do the Bible instruct us to draw closer to God?

3. In what ways have you begun drawing closer to God?

Additional Notes

Additional Notes

Additional Notes

Additional Notes

Journal Entry #3

God's Hand Revealed

"For all this I considered in my heart even to declare all this, that the righteous, and the wise, and their works, are in the hand of God."—Ecclesiastes 9:1

I'VE ALWAYS BEEN FASCINATED WITH THE SKY AND ALL the beautiful colors in nature. I remember one day remarking about how breathtakingly beautiful the sky - and all of nature - is. I asked myself, "I wonder if God made the sky and everything in nature the colors they are?" That same night, while asleep, I had a vision of an open sky before me. In this vision, I saw a massive hand; it was God's hand! He didn't have a paint brush in His hand; instead, He just moved His hand across the sky, and the colors appeared. I just watched as His hand moved, and at that moment, I realized that God is an artist.

God knew my thoughts. He heard my inner thoughts

concerning how beautiful the sky was. In the vision, He told me to write down everything I saw, which I did after I woke up. Now, I'm even more excited about looking up and beholding the beauty and glory of the first heaven (the sky), which the Lord takes great pleasure in painting with His finger. As the Word of God declares in Genesis 1:1, "In the beginning God created the heavens and the earth." God is creative. He loves to create. He is the source of all of the beauty we see in the earth. It was all done by His hand.

Another day, God revealed His hand to me once again. This time, just like before, He had given me an open vision while I was in bed. In this vision, I saw a Bible. It was open before me. Suddenly, I saw a hand appear and began turning the pages. The hand was turning the pages so fast I could barely keep up. Before this vision, I had started praying for God to speak to me about His purpose for my life. I was praying and asking Him to reveal to me what He called me to do in this world. Suddenly, in this vision, the hand landed on a verse of Scripture in Genesis 1:27, which says, "We were made in God's image. In the image of God he created them; male and female he created them" (NIV). The interesting thing about the hands I saw turning the pages is they weren't very different from our hands. The only difference between those hands and ours is the skin color. I was amazed to see this although I was still left with the question of my purpose in life. I would later discover that the way God works is He reveals different revelations about our purposes at different times in our lives and through different circumstances. The hand of the Lord is at work in our lives even though we can't see everything God is doing, but in due time, He reveals all things. Sometimes, He does so little

GOD'S HAND REVEALED

by little.

God kept revealing His hand in my life in little ways. For example, one week, my cousin came down from Arizona to visit his dad (my uncle). We were at my grandmother's house, hanging out in the kitchen. I was about to leave for the night when grandma stopped me and asked me to pray. I didn't know what to pray for, but I told God I would listen to hear what He had to say. When I started praying, I felt a sudden wind blow in the kitchen where we were. I knew that was the presence of the Lord in our midst. That mysterious wind blew through grandma's kitchen, and we all found ourselves under the power of God. I heard a voice say at that moment, "I've called this family to preach the Gospel." That voice shook my insides. I knew that it was God. I heard tongues of a different language in my head, and then I heard God's voice speaking—his audible voice in English. It scared me at first, but I knew that I had nothing to be afraid of. He said in His Word, "If two or more are gathered in my name he would be in our midst" (Matthew 18:20, NIV).

God revealed His hand in my life through the different circumstances I experienced. For example, I remember getting hurt on my job. Behind this, I was given time off. I spent those ten months believing God for a miracle. I had lost my new car during this time due to not being able to pay my car note. I wasn't receiving any compensation from my job at this time, and my unemployment was about to run out. My family helped me as much as they could. I was down to about fifty dollars a week income. Times were rough, and the only person I could lean on was my Savior, Jesus Christ. I don't recall ever crying so much in my life. I had a son to take care. So I knew that there was no way God had forgot-

ANSWER THE CALL

ten about me. I cried out to Him, "Where are you? Please God, don't forget about me! Please!" I fell asleep, and there I was, standing in what looked like a hurricane outside. I was getting rained on. The wind was blowing very hard. I then heard a voice say,

"Praise God through your storm." I began to raise my hands in the air in my dream. I started to praise God, singing to Him from my heart. Suddenly, the clouds began to move away, and there He was, the face of my Savior; it was Jesus! I noticed that the wind stopped blowing and the rain stopped falling. Even in my dreams, Jesus calmed the storm. He calmed my storm. As I looked up in the sky, Jesus smiled at me, and I smiled back. His eyes were filled with love. There are no other words to describe it. This peace came over me, and I felt loved. Jesus had a beard, and His hair was mid-length and bronze looking. It looked as if He had highlights. His eyes were that of a bluish-green color, and they appeared big to me. They were filled with so much love... that the tears wouldn't stop falling from my eyes. He calmed the internal storm I was experiencing during that time while jobless and stressed. God knows what you are going through. He knows everything we go through—everything! He loves you so much! Lean on Him. Turn to Him. Call upon Him. Furthermore, trust in Him. His hand is on your life, and He's going to see you through.

Your Time To Reflect

1. Have you asked God to reveal to you His will for your life?

GOD'S HAND REVEALED

If so, in what ways has He spoken to you?

2. When you look at nature (the sky, trees, grass, flowers, etc.), you can see the hand-print of God. In what ways has God revealed Himself through His own creation?

Additional Notes

Additional Notes

Additional Notes

Journal Entry #4

The Trust Game

"Trust in the Lord with all thine heart; and lean not unto thine own understanding…"—Proverbs 3:5

During the I was out of work, I received a supernatural visitation. Jesus appeared to me. The only thing He said to me was, "Follow me." He was moving so fast that I could only see the back Him and His robe. We were in what looked like a maze, a race. We were almost running. It was a course that went up and down, left and right. At the end of the course, there was a door. When we reached the door, Jesus disappeared. Other people were coming out of the door. I went through the door and found myself standing outside. It was like the dawn before the dusk. I saw clouds all over the ground. There was a light that was coming through the sky; I thought it was the sun, but it wasn't. It was a large cross coming towards me, and it had yellow illuminating

ANSWER THE CALL

light radiating from it. I was drawn to it, and I began to be pulled towards it as it hovered in the air. The closer I got to it, the more I felt a warm feeling all over me. I could feel the power of the cross the closer I got to it. I could feel this the warmth, the power of that cross both inside of me and all over my body. I could feel its power and strength. I almost touched the cross, and then suddenly, I began to fall backward from the cross. Suddenly, I was descending from the sky in a free-fall. While falling, I felt a pair of hands on my back, catching me; those hands were so gentle and loving. Immediately, I woke up, gasping for air. Tears were running down my face; I was breathing so hard. Just then, I heard the Lord say in my spirit, "Peace, my daughter. Peace."

Sometimes we feel as if we're falling, spiraling downward towards doom and destruction with no way of escape. Sometimes we find ourselves stressing and worrying about things and thinking God has abandoned us, but in reality, He is right there beside us. He has to teach us how to trust and follow Him, how to rely on His ability to guide and lead us and know that He is there to catch us when we fall. We are never alone. Know and believe that. You are never alone. God not only sees you in your time of need, but He has a plan for you in your time of need. Trust Him.

Your Time To Reflect

1. God has to teach us how to relax and trust Him in our lives. This isn't always easy, but it's necessary. In what ways can you say God has or is teaching you how to trust in Him?

THE TRUST GAME

2. In what ways do we demonstrate our trust in God?

Additional Notes

Additional Notes

Additional Notes

Journal Entry #5

Your Miracle Is Here

"Jesus said unto him, If thou canst believe, all things are possible to him that believeth."—Mark 9:23

THERE I WAS, INJURED AND IN NEED OF HEALING myself, but I was praying for others to receive a healing, a miracle from God. One night, while praying for a sick family member, I remember uttering out loud, "God, where are you?" I tend to ask Him that question when in need of a miracle. He perhaps sensed the humor and irony in that question considering that it was He who woke me up that night. When the Lord woke me up, He replayed that question in my head; instead of His voice, however, it was my voice playing back at me as if being played through a tape recorder. There it was, my voice, my words: "God, where are you?" Just then, in a vision, I saw a dark open sky before me; it looked like nighttime. I could see the stars. I then saw Jesus' face. He was looking down at me while I was looking up at Him in the sky. He appeared to be searching for something. My voice echoed through my mind once more: "God, where are you?" Then Jesus' face was so close to mine that I was startled and speechless. We were now standing face to face. I said, "Jesus!" We made direct eye contact. He had the most beautiful eyes I had ever see. I woke up right after that.

    Not too long after that encounter with Jesus, I went to the altar to receive prayer. Pastor Keith Ford prayed for me concerning the two things that had been on my mind: my divine purpose in life and my injured foot that needed surgery. It had been almost eighteen months, and I needed to know that God didn't forget about me. He was quiet. I hadn't had any supernatural encounters lately. I was down and out, out of work due to my injury, and I needed to know that God still heard my prayers. I needed a miracle from Him because I was now broke. I had no income and couldn't pay my bills. Suddenly, God did come through for me. I received two miracles reminding me that God had not forgotten about me. After the service where Pastor Ford prayed for me, I went to get some food. Although Pastor had prayed for me during the church service, I didn't immediately feel any different. I still didn't have any feeling in my left foot, and I was still afraid that I'd have to have foot surgery, which I didn't want to get. I still could not bend my toes or wiggle them due to my accident—a car crushed my foot while at work. The doctor told me that I would need surgery to remove a damaged nerve that was between my second and third toe; this meant permanent foot damage. I was informed that I would never wear heels again and I would have to wear specially made shoes for the rest of my life. However, I believed God could heal me, and I was not about to give up my high heels.

My son and I were in the drive-through at the fast food restaurant when, all of a sudden, my left foot began to tingle. I took off my shoe and tried to wiggle my toes. I was suddenly able to move and bend them. God healed my foot! I could now wear high heels again, and I didn't need surgery done on my foot! Hallelujah!

Later that night, while still pumped from the first miracle God had just performed on my foot, I saw a bright light appeared in my room. At first, I thought it was the bathroom light—I'd normally leave my bedroom door slightly opened, which would allow the bathroom light to penetrate my room. However, this wasn't the bathroom light. This light was much brighter. At that moment, I heard the voice of the Lord speak to me and say, "For I know the plans I have for you." The sound of God's voice startled me so until I could hardly catch my breath. Tears poured down my face. These were tears of joy, of happiness, of relief through knowing that God loves me and He heard my prayers all along during those times when I thought He was absent or ignoring me. He doesn't have a certain time to visit us. He doesn't move when we want Him to. But when He does visit us, when He does move, His presence and power are unmistakable.

God reminded me of His promise in Jeremiah 29:11. He knows our beginning and our end. He knows our thoughts before we think them.

ANSWER THE CALL

Your Time To Reflect

1. God is a miracle working God. He has the ability to heal us of any sickness and disease that may come upon us. Do you believe in the miracle working power of God? If so, what examples from the Bible provides evidence of God's miracle working power?

YOUR MIRACLE IS HERE

2. What areas in your life do you need a miracle in? (Write them down and believe God for a miracle in these areas)

Additional Notes

Additional Notes

Additional Notes

Journal Entry #6
Lucifer

"How art thou fallen from heaven, O Lucifer, son of the morning!"—Isaiah 14:12

God allowed me to see Lucifer, the fallen angel, in a dream one night. He is cunning. I was walking with one of my sisters in my dream. I still don't know where we were and why we were walking, but the vision was so vivid. I remember a car pulling up to us, and what looked like a tall angel stepped out of the car. This angel's face was distorted; it had on beautiful garments, but they were dirty. At first, I thought it was an angel until it stretched out its hand and I saw it had snake-like skin and black nails. I jumped back and said, "In the name of Jesus, you devil, leave here!" I repeated myself, and this time, he disappeared.

The devil tried to trick me even in my dream. His job

ANSWER THE CALL

is to steal, kill, and destroy. Jesus came so that we may have life and have it more abundantly.

I've had quite a few encounters with Satan's helpers. I call them Satan's helpers because they are fallen angels who will never return from whence they came. They are demons now, and they will try and use fear as a way to control us while we're asleep. I've heard older people describe nighttime demonic attacks as feeling like witches are riding your back or something to that effect. Well, I've seen them first hand, and yes, at the name of Jesus they must leave also. Most of the time, they would wait until I was asleep to attack me. God allowed me to go through this so that I would be able to help others who're going through the same thing. I knew that there was a calling on my life because the closer I got to God, the more Satan would try and bother me; I just wasn't sure at the time what my calling was. I've rebuked and sent many demons back to hell in Jesus' name. I've had them breathe in my face, even talk, and I could see some through the eyes of the spirit. Their fear tactics don't work on me anymore because I now know what I am called to do. I must do it quickly! Anytime these things happen to you, rebuke these demons in Jesus' name and tell them to go. For God has not given us the spirit of fear (2 Timothy 1:7).

Your Time To Reflect

1. Satan and his demons are real. Jesus talked a lot about them and explained to us that we would be able to cast them out in His name. But before we can take authority over our

LUCIFER

adversary, we must first recognize our adversary. Take a moment and write down the different names given to Satan in God's Word.

2. Satan attacks us because he knows God has great plans in store for us. In what ways has Satan began attacking your life that you can recognize?

Additional Notes

Additional Notes

Additional Notes

Journal Entry #7
My Visit To Hell

"And if thy foot offend thee, cut it off: it is better for thee to enter halt into life, than having two feet to be cast into hell, into the fire that never shall be quenched."—Mark 9:45

One night, God had allowed me to see heaven in a dream. In my dream, I saw several of my family members there; they looked so happy, so peaceful. However, I remember asking God why I wasn't seeing one particular family member who had passed away there. I sincerely missed seeing this person and much desired to see them again in heaven; but one morning, God allowed me to see this person. They were not in Heaven; they were in Hell. As I walked up to what looked like a jail cell, I saw the soul of this person there. I gasped! I then heard them say, "God, I'm so sorry. I'm so sorry, Lord." I called the person's name, but they could not hear me. They were in a cell with their head down, and I could see the dimmest light. There was fire from the flames of their soul, and they would be there forever. I cried,

"God, I didn't ask to see that!"

That is what happens when we don't accept Jesus. Hell is real, and to see someone that I loved there who had been given the opportunity to live for Jesus was heart-wrenching. It was rough for me to see that, but I had to write it down; for this was part of my purpose, too.

Your Time To Reflect

1. Jesus talked more about Hell than He did Heaven in the Bible. Why do you think that is so?

MY VISIT TO HELL

2. What does the Bible say about Hell and how to avoid going to that place?

Additional Notes

Additional Notes

Additional Notes

Journal Entry #8

A Place Called Heaven

"How that he was caught up into paradise, and heard unspeakable words, which it is not lawful for a man to utter."
—2 Corinthians 12:4

I DREAMED OF MY AUNTIE TODAY. SHE IS MY MOTHER'S sister, my favorite aunt in all the whole world. She was a precious jewel that gave freely and would help anyone that was in need. I miss her presence!

Just as before, God has shown me in a dream my aunt. She was in heaven, unlike the other family member God showed me. I knew this was Heaven. This place was unmistakable and drastically different from Hell. It had beautiful tropical looking trees, and the flowers seemed to dance, swaying from side to side. The colors in that place were so vibrant they seem to come alive. Up there was my aunt. The brightness of that place was so intense I had to squint my eyes to see. I saw my aunt. She was standing there talking within a group of people; she looked so beautiful. Everyone had robes on. Heaven is so beautiful it's indescribable. I am thankful for the glimpse of Heaven God allowed me to see.

On another occasion, I saw my aunt. She asked me if I was okay in this dream. She took my hand and squeezed it. I felt warm all over, and tears began to fall from my eyes. I could feel her squeeze my hand. I truly miss her beautiful spirit.

In another dream, I saw my grandmother's father sitting in a white chair in an all-white room. He looked the same as the day he died, but a little younger in the face. He nicknamed me TT as a child, and in my dream, he asked me if I was okay? He took my hand and squeezed it just like my aunt did in my other dream, and it felt real. I just hugged him while crying tears of joy. He would always say, "I love you TT, and I love all my grandchildren." I remember we would always watch cowboys and Indians. He loved westerns. He would let me sit in his chair where I'd fall asleep. He would always take my hand in his and pat it. "I love you, TT. I love all of my grandchildren."

I miss my Gramps. He had the most beautiful eyes and curly, wavy hair. I can picture him now in his overalls.

Your Time To Reflect

1. Just like Hell, Jesus talked about Heaven in the Bible. Heaven is mentioned in other passages of Scripture as well. What does the Bible say about Heaven?

A PLACE CALLED HEAVEN

2. What does the Bible say is the only way to get to Heaven?

Additional Notes

Additional Notes

Additional Notes

Journal Entry #9

A Child Found

"Take heed that ye despise not one of these little ones; for I say unto you, That in heaven their angels do always behold the face of my Father which is in heaven."—Matthew 18:10

IN IN 2008, I WAS PREGNANT WITH A BABY GIRL. I DIDN'T know that it was a girl until God allowed me to see her one day under the most unusual circumstances. I had a miscarriage on November 1, 2008, during my first trimester and lost my baby girl. That was one of the most challenging things I ever had to go through. However, one day, God allowed me to see my baby girl in a dream. In my dream, I was at my grandma's house. While there, a beautiful little girl walked up to me while I was sitting on a couch. She had on a pink shirt, blue jeans, and wore a crown on her head with jewels in it. She was trying to pull herself up on the sofa beside me like a typical toddler would do. Her steps were kind of wobbly, and she needed help to reach the couch. I was amazed at how beautiful she was. Without realizing at first that she was my daughter, I said to her, "Your hair is so pretty." She responded,

"My auntie did it, mommy."

"Where is your auntie?" I asked here. It still hadn't dawned on me that she was my baby girl and that the aunt she was referring to was my mom's sister who had gone to be with Jesus four years prior. I didn't realize that she was my daughter until she called my aunt's name. My aunt was seeing after my baby, the daughter that I miscarried. I woke up and cried.

I miss my baby and my aunt. I know now that she is in good hands. If you have ever lost a baby, know that they are in Heaven being looked after by family. My aunt was the most beautiful spirited woman you'd ever know.

Your Time To Reflect

1. With an epidemic of abortions in our nation and so many other causes of death plaguing our children, it's important to know that no soul is lost. The souls of babies go back to Heaven from whence they came. How does this revelation impact you?

A CHILD FOUND

2. What does this revelation say about death in general?

Additional Notes

Additional Notes

Additional Notes

Journal Entry #10
God Disappointed

"For unto whomsoever much is given, of him shall be much required…"—Luke 12:48

WE SHOULD NEVER BE TOO BUSY TO TAKE the time out to pray and have our daily devotion. This day, God wasn't happy with me. I'd been lazy. I hadn't read my Bible and prayed in a while. This morning, God woke me up and uttered these words in my spirit: "I'm disappointed in you." Ouch! That hurt. I immediately jumped out of bed and got on my knees and asked God to please forgive me for pretending as if I was too busy to spend time with Him. He made time for me, so why couldn't I make the time for Him? In plus, I'd been begging Him to show me my purpose, what I am supposed to be doing if life.

Never be too busy to pray, worship, and go to church. If you do so, God will get your attention one way or another!

Your Time To Reflect

1. Just because you love someone, that doesn't mean their actions can't disappoint you. Although God loves us all, He gets disappointed just like we do. This has been expressed multiple times throughout the Bible. Can you pinpoint any passages in the Bible where this has happened before?

2. Like any parent, just because God is disappointed with our actions, that doesn't mean He is disappointed with us. Instead, what He desires is that we do differently, not for His sake, but for ours. Why does God want us to do differently?

3. What are the benefits of spending time with God daily?

Additional Notes

Additional Notes

Additional Notes

Journal Entry #11
In My Face

"But if ye forgive not men their trespasses, neither will your Father forgive your trespasses."—Matthew 6:15

I thought I had forgiven everyone who had ever done me wrong, but God proved me wrong on this day. God searches our hearts since out of the heart flows the issues of life.

It had been many years since one particular person hurt me. I was trying to be cordial with them. However, one day, a thought ran across my mind about this individual. I said to myself I would never forgive them for what they did to me. I didn't think God was paying attention to that statement, but He was. I just went on throughout my day after that. When nighttime came, I prepared for bed. Suddenly, I'd fallen asleep. Suddenly, while sleeping, I found myself standing outside of my body. I could see my room, and my body still laying in the bed. The curtains began to blow and move. I could feel the wind blowing in my face. Then it started to get warm. As I stood there, I could hear a deep and stern voice. This voice was different from Jesus' voice. I knew that it was the Heavenly Father's voice. He said, "Forgive and let it go!" He spoke this about five times. While He spoke it, I could feel His breath; this is when I truly realized that God knows and sees everything in the deepest core of our existence. I was scared because He took the time to visit me. Quickly, I repented of the unforgiveness I had in my heart towards this person. If that is you, please, I urge you, forgive that person no matter what they did.

Your Time To Reflect

1. What does the Bible say about forgiveness? (Find all of the Bible verses that talk about forgiveness and explain them)

IN MY FACE

2. God said, "Vengeance is mine, saith the Lord" in Romans the 12th chapter. What did God mean by that?

Additional Notes

Additional Notes

Additional Notes

Journal Entry #12

An Angel At My Door

"The angel of the LORD encampeth round about them that fear him, and delivereth them."—Psalm 34:7

I HAVE A HABIT OF GOING TO THE BATHROOM IN THE WEE hours of the morning. I usually get up between 3 and 4 am to go to the bathroom; and afterward, I'll climb back into my bed. Usually, at night I'll sleep next to the window, which is on the right side of my bed, and falling back to sleep would be no problem, but not on this night. This time, while I was in bed, I happened to glance over by the door, and as I turned my head back forward, I looked up and noticed a wing stretched out over me from the ceiling. I then looked to my left, and an angel was standing there shining so brightly. Its wings had the most beautiful detail to them. It was a male angel. It wore armor and was huge. He had a sword in his hand as if he was waiting and ready for battle. There was a feeling of incredible peace in my room. I turned and looked away at first, and then turned again in the direction of the angel to see if he'd still be there, and he was, still standing in the same position, watching guard over me as I lay there.

The Word of God tells us God will give His angels charge to watch over us. I thank God that He allowed me to see my angel. I know that even while I'm asleep, I am protected. That's amazing!

Your Time To Reflect

1. The Bible talks a lot about angels. Many of them would appear before men during much needed times. Can you think of a couple of examples in the Bible of angels appearing before men?

2. What are some of the primary tasks of angels you've noticed in the Bible?

3. Have you ever had an encounter with an angel?

Additional Notes

Additional Notes

Additional Notes

Journal Entry #13
Angelic Intervention

"The angel of the LORD encampeth round about them that fear him, and delivereth them."—Psalm 91:11

A WHILE BACK, I USE TO WORK THE THIRD SHIFT on a job. I would have to drive about 30 minutes to get home to Morrow, Georgia at the time. One particular morning, instead of me stopping by my mom's house to take a quick nap before hitting the road like I usually did after work, I proceeded to drive on home. About ten minutes into the trip home I fell asleep behind the wheel. I didn't realize that I'd fallen asleep. I ended up crossing over into oncoming traffic. My car had completely crossed the opposite lane, and by the time I knew it, I was in a ditch getting to hit a huge sign. While asleep, I felt someone shake me. I instantly woke up, only to end up in a state of horror and panic, shocked and feeling scared to death. I felt like I was about to die because the car was still going full speed and I was yards away from hitting a large construction sign. I screamed "Jesus!" and then attempted to hit the brakes, but I knew the car wouldn't slow down in time to keep me from missing the sign. All, of a sudden, I felt someone touch my foot and press harder on the brake, and miraculously, the car began to slow down; the steering wheel started to stabilize. I then noticed that there was another individual in the car with me, and it was an angel. When the car stopped, it was directly in front of the construction sign. Not one scratch was on my car, and I wasn't even hurt. At the speed the car was going, I would have been ejected out of the vehicle on impact and died. Amazingly, after catching my breath, I was able to maneuver and drive out of the ditch. Thank God! He sent his angel to look after me again. .

Your Time To Reflect

1. In what ways have God's angels protected you? Can you think of any?

ANGELIC INTERVENTION

Additional Notes

Additional Notes

Additional Notes

Journal Entry #14
Angels Singing With Us

"And suddenly there was with the angel a multitude of the heavenly host praising God, and saying, Glory to God in the highest, and on earth peace, good will toward men.."
—Luke 2:13-14

I STARTED TO FELLOWSHIP WITH OTHER FELLOW Christian women from various churches and backgrounds. Twice a year, we would fellowship at the women's retreat in Blue Ridge, Georgia, in the mountains. This retreat was like no other retreat I'd ever experienced. This time, I could not only feel the presence of angels, but I could hear them singing. They were singing beautifully while we were singing and worshiping. At that retreat, it was about eighty women there, but it sounded like hundreds of people were singing with us. I could only hear the angels singing with us, but another lady testified that she saw them singing with us.

ANSWER THE CALL

It was an incredible experience!

Your Time To Reflect

1. In the Bible, angels are described as standing around God's throne worshiping Him. Angels love to worship God. Just like angels, we were also created to worship God. In what ways do the angels worship God in the Bible? What do they say and do as an act of worship?

2. Why is it important that we worship God in our daily lives?

Additional Notes

Additional Notes

Additional Notes

Journal Entry #15
Heaven Invading The Room

". . . so that the priests could not stand to minister because of the cloud, for the glory of the LORD filled the house of God."
—2 Chronicles 5:14

FRIDAY NIGHT WORSHIP SERVICES DOWN IN Williamson, Georgia, were amazing. You can still find me there most Friday nights. They call it the Tabernacle. I began to witness God reveal Himself at these services in ways I'd never seen before. During worship, most times I'll close my eyes while in deep praise. During these moments, I'd picture angels dancing to the music. Once at the ladies retreat, while my eyes were closed I could see them up front during worship. I could see their wings swaying to the music.

We were created for worship. Everything was made for God's glory. After opening my eyes and then closing them, and then opening them again, I could see the angels even clearer. I could see colors from Heaven during worship. It was like the building didn't have a roof on it, and Heaven's light was shining down through the open roof. The angels appeared with Jesus as He walked among us.

Your Time To Reflect

1. Psalm 22:3 tells us God "inhabits the praises" of His people. What does it mean to "inhabit" something?

2. If the Bible tells us God inhabits the praises of His people, then what does that mean to you and I?

HEAVEN INVADING THE ROOM

Additional Notes

Additional Notes

Additional Notes

Journal Entry #16

A Heart for Africa

"Go ye therefore, and teach all nations, baptizing them in the name of the Father, and of the Son, and of the Holy Ghost…"
—*Matthew 28:19*

I'VE ALWAYS HAD A HEART FOR THE POOR CHILDREN living in different countries. When I was small, and I would see a television commercial asking for aid for the impoverished children in other lands, I would ask my mom if we could bring one of those kids home. Sometimes, while at my grandparents' house during the summer, when those television commercials would air, I'd ask my Gramps if we could bring one of those children home. God placed a burning desire in my heart to help others as a child. When I became an adult, I had the opportunity to sponsor two kids from Uganda, Africa, through a ministry that had connections there. The ministry was based out of Jackson, Georgia.

ANSWER THE CALL

I sponsored a girl, then later, a boy.

Ten other ladies and I signed up to go to Uganda, Africa, to do missionary work. We met with the pastors at the ministry in Jackson, Georgia. They had been to Uganda, Africa, to minister before. They showed us clips of the kids in Africa. We were going to conduct a week-long Vacation Bible School with the kids from an orphanage there that was being run by a pastor and his wife. God placed within their hearts a desire to take in kids off of the streets that were homeless. Some of these kids' parents had died in accidents. Some of the kids were taking care of their younger siblings as if their parents were dead or had abandoned them. It was sad; this melted my heart.

The pastors explained to us what was required of us to make the trip. They told us about the financial cost, the shots we needed to take, the hotel, and more. Out of the ten ladies who signed up, only two of us were able to go. Unfortunately, I was one of the ones who were unable to make it mainly due to finances. Even still, I knew that this wasn't the end of the road for me. I asked God to show me a sure sign that it was meant for me to go.

Your Time To Reflect

1. The Bible tells us in Philippians 2:13 that God both works within us to desire His will and to do His will. This is interesting because it reveals to us that God will give us a burning desire to do the things that He already intends for us

to do when we seek Him and spend time with Him. Oftentimes, we are praying for God to reveal to us His will for our lives when He has already spoken to our hearts. What desires have God placed in your heart? What passion or passions have God given you to pursue in this life for His glory?

2. Whenever you gain or develop a passion for something and you perceive this to be a sign from God that this is what He wants you to do in life, it is important to ask God to confirm His will to you, and know that He will speak to you in various ways to confirm His will.

Additional Notes

Additional Notes

Additional Notes

Journal Entry #17
God Shows Me Africa

"Then was the secret revealed unto Daniel in a night vision. Then Daniel blessed the God of heaven."—Daniel 2:19

A FEW MONTHS HAD PASSED, AND I WAS carrying on with life as usual. I was still thinking heavily about going back to Africa and was sponsoring kids, but I felt like I needed to do more. The burning desire to do missionary work in Africa never departed out of my heart.

One night, after I finished praying, I fell asleep. While asleep, I dreamed I was on an airplane heading to a foreign destination, a place I was unfamiliar with. When I glanced out of my window, I noticed we were beginning to land. I started to wonder to myself, 'Where am I going?' The place looked beautiful from the window. I looked around on the plane, and I didn't see any familiar faces.

After the plane landed, we got off the plane. As far as

ANSWER THE CALL

I could see, people were waving and yelling, "We are so glad you made it to the homeland!" While I was walking, a lady approached me and said,

"Welcome, daughter! I am so glad you are here." She gave me a drink as if she knew I was thirsty. I realized then that I was in Africa. I could tell by the way the people dressed. I saw women carrying baskets of food on top of their heads. I suddenly noticed that I had a Bible in my hand. I then heard the Lord say,

"Preach to the people about my kingdom."

In the dream, I was with a team, and we were going door to door praying and doing crusade work. Later, I saw myself standing on a stage in front of an endless amount of people stretching back as far as the eye could see. There was seemingly no end. There were lines of people waiting to get prayed for as well. Suddenly, we were standing in a field, and there was a long line of people on my left. When I looked to my right, I noticed an airplane. After that, I immediately woke up.

Even as a child, God was speaking to me about my calling in life through those television commercials, and now He was beginning to confirm in my spirit through dreams what I had started to sense was His calling for my life.

I don't question whether or not God exists. I know He does. Whenever I have questions about anything, I can take them to God, and He speaks to me concerning the matters of my heart. I never asked God to choose me, but I know it is an honor to be chosen by Him and to do the work He has called me to do. I have the utmost fear and respect for God because he is a great God. All of the concerns I had about going to Africa, in the beginning, are no longer there

GOD SHOWS ME AFRICA

because I gained the revelation that that's where I belong—it is God's will for me to be there.

God has always been there, speaking to me, whispering into my spirit His plans for my life in subtle ways. He's been there from day one.

Your Time To Reflect

1. Has God ever confirmed His will for your life? If so, how has He spoken to you and confirmed His will for you?

Additional Notes

Additional Notes

Additional Notes

Journal Entry #18

My Calling Revealed

"In the mouth of two or three witnesses shall every word be established."—2 Corinthians 13:1

IN THE SUMMER OF 2015, MY CALLING WAS REVEALED TO me in such a specific way. I knew then that everything I'd ever gone through in my life was for this purpose. My life, my surroundings, my location, and even the family I was born into was for my God-given assignment. How could I think I could escape the call to preach? "Me, Lord? Little ole' me?" I wondered. I often asked why me, but then the thought came to mind, "Why not me?"

I'd always known that God existed even as a little girl. When I came to know Jesus in such an intimate way, He changed my life—He revealed to me who He was; this would then explain why my mom's pregnancy was different with me than with my sister, and it would also explain why I felt so out of place in school and why I never felt like I fit in. God would not allow me to do what everyone else did. Of course, I tried to drink, party, smoke, but I would end up so miserable and empty inside.

On that particular day, God revealed to me my future. It was a vision of my future. I was standing behind a pulpit. I had to look twice because I thought it was my mom—after all, we do look alike. It was me, and God said to me, "Your job is to preach to the people about my Kingdom." He spoke those words to me with great authority. As I looked out into the congregation, I heard the Father speak in my ear, and everything He'd say I'd repeat it. I looked back at myself, and I saw a cloud cover the place, and while I was speaking people started falling all over the place like dominoes. I could feel God's power and strength. I then said,

"God I will get the message out. I will be obedient to what you've called me to do".

There was a second confirmation from God regarding my calling that same year at the Tabernacle. I was walking through the prayer line (or "fire tunnel," which was a prophetic prayer line people would walk through where the ministers, pastors, and prophets would pray and prophecy over you as you walked through) when all eight of the ministers ministering gave me almost the same word from God. They all revealed to me that I was called to reach the masses—millions of people. I said to myself, "Lord, I don't have the power to do it." However, God later assured me that it wasn't my power that I'd be operating in; it was His power I had to rely on and operate within.

MY CALLING REVEALED

Your Time To Reflect

1. Oftentimes, when God speaks to us about His will for our lives, He'll confirm it through the mouths of his servants, the prophets. God may speak through your Pastor, through one of the ministers at your church, or send a prophet your way. Many times, God will tell you to get up and go to a church or prayer meeting where He has already placed a word concerning your life and situation in the mouth of one of His ministers there. We must position ourselves to hear and receive from God. What are a few things the Bible tells us to do to position ourselves where we can hear and receive from God?

2. When God speaks to us about His purpose for our lives, it's usually something too big for us to handle on our own

ANSWER THE CALL

without His power, strength, and ability. God always gives us a dream that's too big for us to handle on our own. We serve a God who specializes in doing the extraordinary through ordinary people. What big dream or dreams has God given you?

3. What does it mean to rely on God's power? What does the Bible teach about trusting and relying on God?

MY CALLING REVEALED

Additional Notes

Additional Notes

Additional Notes

Prayer

If you don't know Jesus invite him into your heart. Don't be like the family member I saw in Hell! To welcome Him into your heart, just pray this prayer:

> Please repeat after me! Lord Jesus, I admit that I am a sinner. I ask you to forgive me of my sins. I believe that you died for my sins and, that you rose again on the third day. I ask you to come into my heart and be my Lord and Savior. Cleanse me from all unrighteousness! I ask you to come into my heart and be my Lord and Savior. Fill me with your precious Holy Spirit and, live in me now. You said if we confess our sins, you are faithful and just to forgive us, and cleanse us from all unrighteousness. My past has been erased, and my sins have been forgiven. Forgive me, Father! From this day forth I will never be the same! In Jesus' name! Amen!

If you prayed this prayer, then I want to welcome into the family of God!

ABOUT THE AUTHOR

Debrecia is a follower of Jesus Christ. She desires to write what the Father has placed on her heart through dreams and visions. She has worked extensively in ministry, serving on the youth street outreach team in Griffin, Georgia, and in the ministry internship for Voice to the Nations. She also volunteers for Prison Fellowship Ministries in Georgia.

Debrecia has a Bachelors degree from Argosy University, and she has over seven years of experience as business owner and marketing strategist. She is the owner and CEO of Higher Connections Personnel for customer service contract jobs. She is also the owner of Breeze Angel Perfume, which is her fragrance line.

Debrecia loves to travel, spend time with family, and go to the beach. Her passion in life is to let people know that God is real and that His mercies are new every day. Her favorite scripture is Jeremiah 29:11, which reads, "For I know the plans I have for you."

Debrecia resides in Griffin, Georgia, with her husband, Michael, her son, Caeland, and her two step-daughters, Michelle and Makla.

To contact author, go to:
debrecia@outlook.com
Facebook: Debrecia Echols
Instagram: @debrecia
Twitter: @debrecia_echols

www.ingramcontent.com/pod-product-compliance
Lightning Source LLC
Chambersburg PA
CBHW061221070526
44584CB00029B/3923